A Crabtree Branches Book

TOP HIGH SCHOOL SPORTS

BASEBALL

Thomas Kingsley Troupe

Crabtree Publishing
crabtreebooks.com

School-to-Home Support for Caregivers and Teachers

This high-interest book is designed to motivate striving students with engaging topics while building fluency, vocabulary, and an interest in reading. Here are a few questions and activities to help the reader build upon his or her comprehension skills.

Before Reading:

- *What do I think this book is about?*
- *What do I know about this topic?*
- *What do I want to learn about this topic?*
- *Why am I reading this book?*

During Reading:

- *I wonder why...*
- *I'm curious to know...*
- *How is this like something I already know?*
- *What have I learned so far?*

After Reading:

- *What was the author trying to teach me?*
- *What are some details?*
- *How did the photographs and captions help me understand more?*
- *Read the book again and look for the vocabulary words.*
- *What questions do I still have?*

Extension Activities:

- *What was your favorite part of the book? Write a paragraph on it.*
- *Draw a picture of your favorite thing you learned from the book.*

TABLE OF CONTENTS

TOUCH 'EM ALL!

The pitch comes in fast and straight. You wind up and swing. CRACK! The ball sails high and far, past the **infield**. The crowd cheers as it clears the fence. You drop your bat and round the bases. HOME RUN!

Tie up your **cleats** and pull on your cap. We're about to learn why baseball ranks among the TOP HIGH SCHOOL SPORTS.

FUN FACT

Baseball is well known as "America's Favorite Pastime." It is often considered the national sport of the United States.

BASEBALL HISTORY

Baseball was invented in the early 1800s, but forms of the game date back to ancient Egypt. The sport borrows elements from two English games: **cricket** and rounders. In those sports, players use a bat and a ball, too.

Cricket

The first baseball game was played in Hoboken, New Jersey on June 19, 1846.

In the early years of baseball, bases were canvas bags filled with sawdust or sand. The bases were painted white to make them stand out to players. It wasn't until the 1930s that more sturdy bases were used. The new bases had a post underneath that anchored to the ground, keeping them in place.

BASEBALL SEASON

For many high schools in the United States, baseball season starts in mid-March or early April, depending on state and climate. The season typically ends in June.

A baseball game is broken into nine **innings**. Players can expect to play between 20 to 30 games during a high school baseball season.

FUN FACT

Instead of lasting nine innings, early baseball games continued until one team scored 21 runs. Back then, runs were called "aces."

HIGH SCHOOL BASEBALL TEAMS

High schools usually form at least two baseball teams, depending on school size and student interest. A varsity team is mostly made up of juniors and seniors. The school's best baseball players compete at the varsity level.

Varsity

Junior Varsity

A junior varsity team is built with freshmen and sophomores. At this level, athletes enhance their skills in order to try out for the varsity team in the coming years.

In the late 1800s, some batters used wooden bats with a flattened end. This wider design made it easier to hit the ball. The downside? The bats didn't last as long and tended to break and splinter more easily. Today, most high school teams use longer-lasting aluminum or composite bats.

BASICS OF THE GAME

In each inning, teams take turns at bat and on the field. On the field are nine players. They try to achieve three outs to end the opposing team's turn at bat. The batting team tries to score runs. A pitcher throws the ball to the batter, who tries to hit it. When the ball is hit, the batter runs to each of the bases. They score a run when they reach home plate again.

Each run is one point.

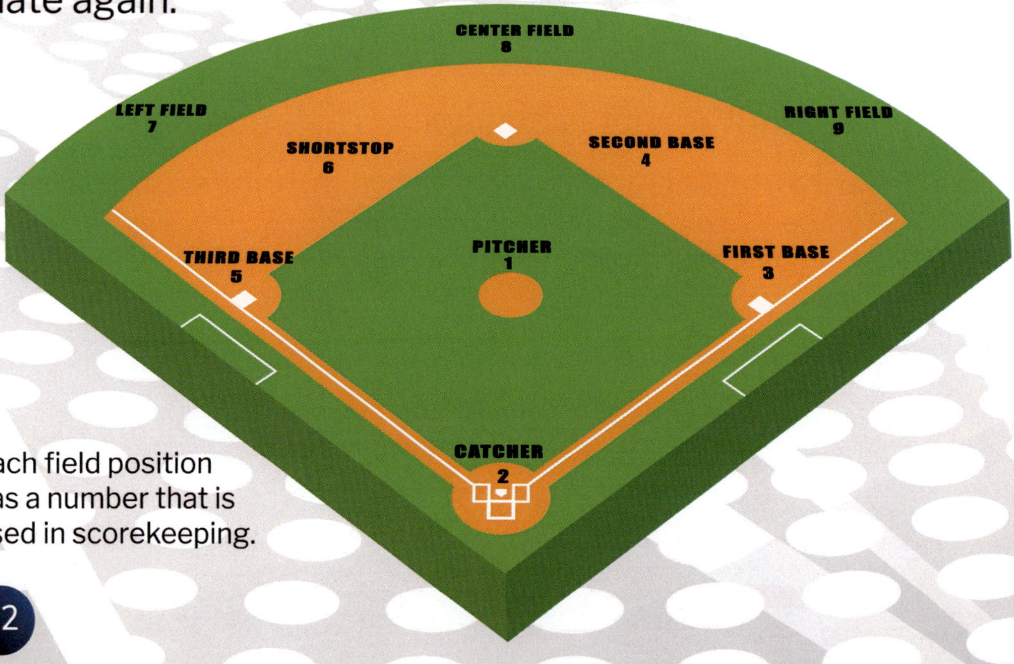

Each field position has a number that is used in scorekeeping.

Swinging and missing the ball is a strike. After three strikes, the player is out. Outs are also achieved when the ball is caught, when a running player is tagged with the ball, or when the ball is thrown to a base before a player reaches it. After three outs, the batting team takes the field.

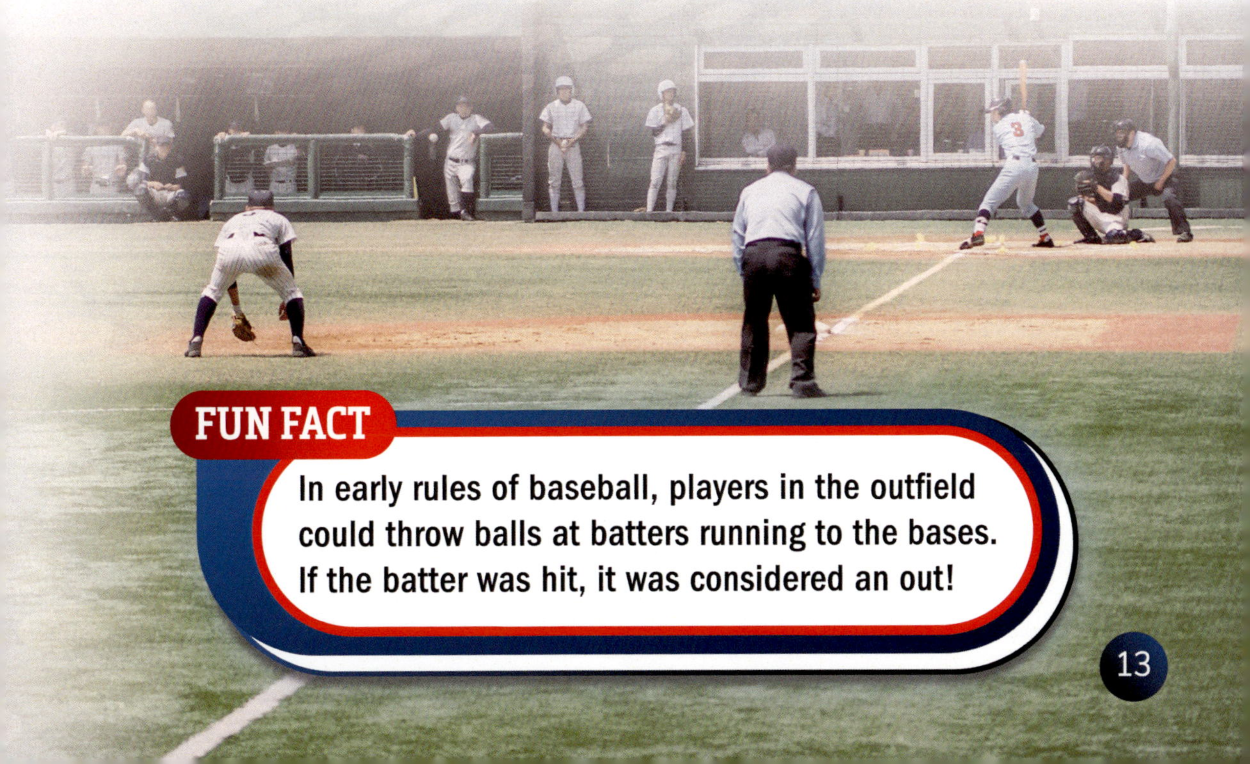

FUN FACT

In early rules of baseball, players in the outfield could throw balls at batters running to the bases. If the batter was hit, it was considered an out!

BASEBALL POSITIONS: PITCHER AND CATCHER

When a baseball team is on defense, or fielding, its goal is to stop the other team from scoring runs. Nine players in total take the field. Each inning starts with the pitcher and catcher.

Pitcher — This player throws, or pitches, the ball to the batter. He or she tries to get the batter to swing and miss the ball. The pitcher stands on the pitcher's mound, in the middle of the diamond.

Catcher — This player crouches at home plate behind the batter. He or she catches any ball the batter misses or does not swing at. The catcher can also tag a runner trying to score a run at home plate.

PITCHER

CATCHER

BASEBALL POSITIONS: BASES

There are four infield players: the first baseman, second baseman, third baseman, and shortstop.

First baseman — This position is one of the most sought-after. A first baseman is probably the player who is thrown to most often. A first baseman must have excellent catching skills.

Second baseman — This player plays between first and second base and is responsible for balls hit in this area. The second baseman shares the duty of covering second base with the shortstop. He or she also shifts their role as needed, depending on the batter.

Third baseman — This player covers third base, which is the last stop before the runner heads to home plate. The third baseman is often a strong thrower who can send a ball across the infield to first base.

Shortstop — This position is played between second and third base. A shortstop handles balls hit in this area and helps cover second base. This player must be a strong catcher and thrower. He or she also helps direct the other infield players.

FIRST BASE

SECOND BASE

SHORTSTOP

THIRD BASE

FUN FACT

Each base is 90 feet (27.43 m) from each other. A home run means the batter will have to run 360 feet (110 m) to reach home plate.

BASEBALL POSITIONS: OUTFIELD

The **outfielders** play an important role on the team, especially when batters knock it out of the infield.

Left field — This player is positioned in the outfield between second and third base. The left fielder needs speed and the ability to catch fly balls, because many are hit into left field.

Center field — This player plays in the middle of the outfield, behind second base. The center fielder is the leader of the outfield. They have to throw farther than any other player.

Right field — This player is positioned in the outfield between first and second base. Because fewer balls tend to be hit to right field, this player also backs up first base.

LEFT FIELD

CENTER FIELD

RIGHT FIELD

EQUIPMENT AND UNIFORMS

Baseball players wear a team jersey, pants, and solid-colored stockings. They wear cleats, to help them run in the sand and turf, and a baseball cap.

A baseball player needs a glove for when they take the field. Helmets are worn when they're up at bat. The helmet shields a player's head from speeding baseballs. Male players wear an athletic cup to protect their **groin**.

With speeding pitches and swinging bats to avoid, catchers play in the most dangerous spot on the diamond! They need a lot of gear to stay safe. Catchers wear a helmet with a face mask, a chest protector, and leg guards. The catcher's mitt is bigger than the mitt of any other player. It has extra padding to protect the catcher's hand.

PRACTICE AND TRAINING

Baseball practice is held after school and usually lasts two hours. Players warm up, play catch, practice batting, and work on fielding.

During **preseason**, some players practice at batting cages. This helps them hit the ball more consistently.

BASEBALL JARGON

There are a lot of strange terms, known as jargon, in baseball. Here are some of the most common.

Batter's Box — The boxes on either side of home plate where the batter stands

Down the Pipe — A pitch thrown right in the middle of a strike zone

Foul Ball — When a ball is hit outside the field of play

Grand Slam — When a home run is hit with players on all three bases

Lineup — The order in which players take turns batting

Shutout — When a pitcher or team doesn't allow their opponents to score any runs

Southpaw — A left-handed pitcher

Whiff — When a batter swings and misses a pitch

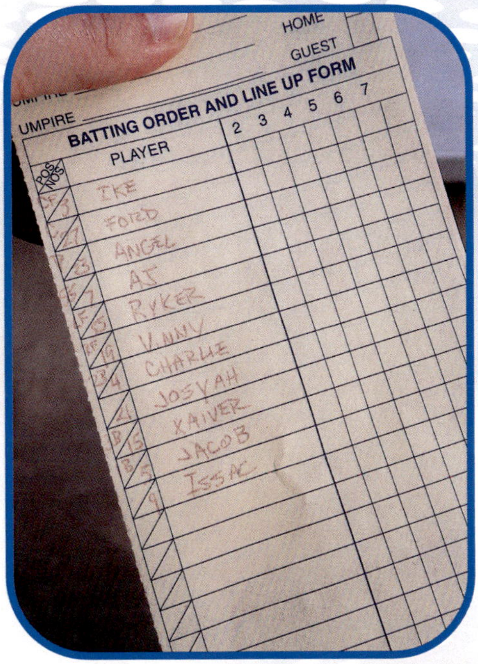

LINEUP

SOUTHPAW

BATTER'S BOX

PLAYOFFS AND STATE TOURNAMENTS

High school baseball teams usually compete with other schools to see which team is the best. Schools can participate in state playoffs and championship **tournaments**.

Like many schools, teams are broken into classes, depending on the number of students enrolled in the high school. Large schools face off against other large schools, while small schools compete against other small schools. This allows for fair competition!

FUN FACT

The fastest pitch ever thrown was by Aroldis Chapman on September 24, 2010. He played for the Cincinnati Reds at the time. His pitch rocketed at an incredible 105.8 miles per hour (170 kph)!

IHSA
2014
BASEBALL
CLASS 4A
STORM
STORM

CONCLUSION

Baseball is one of the most exciting sports for high schoolers. Players will need speed, a sharp eye, and a good arm to keep their team competitive. The practice and hard work is worth it!

Will you hustle out to the diamond with the rest of the players? You and your team could become tournament champions. With a powerful swing and a little patience, you'll see why baseball is easily one of the TOP HIGH SCHOOL SPORTS!

GLOSSARY

aluminum (uh-LOO-muh-nuhm): A lightweight, silvery metal used to make many things

cleats (KLEETS): Special shoes with studs on the bottom to better grip turf or sand

composite (kuhm-POZ-it): Something made up of many things and parts

cricket (KRIK-it): An outdoor team sport played with a bat and ball

groin (GROYN): Area between the abdomen and the thighs

infield (IN-feeld): Area of a baseball field enclosed by the three bases and home plate

innings (IN-ingz): Unit of a baseball or softball game where each team has a turn at bat

outfielders (OWT-feel-drz): Players in the part of the field that is farthest from home plate

preseason (PREE-see-zn): The period of time before a sport's regular season begins

tournaments (TOOR-nuh-muhntz): A series of contests or games played between competing teams

INDEX

WEBSITES TO VISIT

https://www.ducksters.com/sports/baseball.php

https://kids.kiddle.co/Baseball

https://kids.britannica.com/kids/article/baseball/352829

ABOUT THE AUTHOR

Thomas Kingsley Troupe

Thomas Kingsley Troupe is the author of a big ol' pile of books for kids. He's written about everything from ghosts to Bigfoot to third grade werewolves. He even wrote a book about dirt. When he's not writing or reading, he gets plenty of exercise and remembers sacking quarterbacks while on his high school football team. Thomas lives in Woodbury, Minnesota with his two sons.

Written by: Thomas Kingsley Troupe
Designed by: Bobbie Houser
Series Development: James Earley
Editor: Ellen Rodger
Educational Consultant: Marie Lemke M.Ed.
Production manager: Candice Campbell
Prepress technician: Katherine Kantor

Photographs:
t = Top, c = Center, b = Bottom, l = Left, r = Right
Alamy: Colin Waters: p. 6; The Photo Works: p. 7 t; Chronicle: p. 7 b; ZUMA Press: p. 19 tl, p. 22, p. 23 b; Bruce Leighty - Sports Images: p. 19 tr, b, p. 27, p. 28; Marmaduke St. John: p. 23 t
Dreamstime: Mbr Images: cover, p. 17 tr, p. 29 b; Robert Philip: p. 9; Ryo Nagao: p. 10, p. 17 br; Louis Horch: p. 11, p. 17 tl; Dmcdesign: p. 29 t
Shutterstock: David Lee: cover background, p. 1; mTaira: p. 4, p. 5 b, p. 13 b; Joseph Sohm: p. 5 t; tammykayphoto: p. 8; Primo Passo: p. 12 t; Blueberry_8: p. 12 b; JoeSAPhotos: p. 13 t, p. 17 bl, p. 20 l; Cynthia Farmer: p. 15 t; thomas m spindle: p. 15 b; Sean Locke Photography: p. 20 r; New Africa: p. 21 t; ARIES_Studio: p. 24; Red Herring: p. 25 tl; Primo Passo: p. 25 tr; Haslam Photography: p. 25 b

Crabtree Publishing

crabtreebooks.com 800-387-7650

Printed in the U.S.A./CP2025

Published in Canada
Crabtree Publishing
616 Welland Ave.
St. Catharines, Ontario
L2M 5V6

Published in the United States
Crabtree Publishing
347 Fifth Ave
Suite 1402-145
New York, NY 10016

Library and Archives Canada Cataloguing in Publication
Available at Library and Archives Canada

Library of Congress Cataloging-in-Publication Data
Available at the Library of Congress

Hardcover: 978-1-0398-8045-0
Paperback: 978-1-0398-8405-2
Ebook (pdf): 978-1-0398-8165-5
Epub: 978-1-0398-8285-0
Read-Along: 978-1-0398-8429-8
Audio book: 978-1-0398-8423-6